MW01129421

THE ADVENTURES

OF

POLLY THE PENQUIN

Book 1

Written By: Beth Moore

Yellow Light Publishing
P.O. Box 352
Greenwood, DE 19950
www.yellowlightpublishing.com
Ordering information:
For details, contact moore2it@gmail.com
ISBN: 978-0-578-94692-4

This book is dedicated To
My husband, Rick

Without your support and
encouragement, this book would still be
sitting in a drawer waiting for me to
finish it! Your're the best!

TABLE OF CONTENTS

CHAPTER 1
ANTARCTICA

It was another cold, windy day in March. Polly sat at the shore, staring out at the endless ocean. She sometimes shook as each gust of wind pushed its way through her many layers of feathers. Her small penguin body made it a struggle to sit perfectly still in the harsh winds. It was getting colder as the sun was slowly disappearing into the water. She knew it would soon stay dark. This darkness meant many long, cold, and icy days with no sunlight.

Polly closed her eyes and lifted her head as high as she could, soaking up every last drop of sunshine.

She knew this was the last bit of sun for many months to come. Just as the sun sank into the water, Polly heard a familiar voice screeching towards her.

"Watch out!" said Malik, Polly's older brother.

Her eyes were wide open, watching as he jumped straight up out of the water. He put his feet and head up, his flippers out, and slid directly towards her.

"Dude! Shark!" he yelled as he collided with Polly, knocking her feet right out from under her. His massive frame swallowed her up. They began to roll completely out of control until they finally slammed into a huge rock.

"Did you see the mean shark, Polly? He tried to eat me!"

"No, Malik. I didn't see anything, and besides, there are NO sharks here. Now please, get off me!" she said as she struggled to pull herself out from under her brother, chuckling to herself.

Polly was never amused by her brother and his recklessness. In fact, he annoyed Polly most of the time.

He was always goofing off, skipping school, surfing, or anything else to try and look cool. Only on rare occasions would he get into trouble for his silly antics.

He was always doing things he shouldn't do and going places he knew he wasn't allowed to go; tempting fate at every turn. He was determined to prove he was as strong and mighty as his father, almost to a fault.

Polly often found herself wishing she had just a drop of Malik's boldness. Despite what she thought of his antics, Polly truly loved and adored her brother.

Malik climbed his way up to the top of Emperor Hill; which leads to their home. He shook the ice and snow off his feathers while looking down the hill.

"Come on, Polly. It's getting dark. Polly... Polly, are you coming?"

"Yes, I'm coming," she said. "Whatever," she mumbled under her breath as she shrugged her shoulders. She continued to stand there, completely still, gazing out over the water. She could hear Malik in the distance still grumbling to himself about the vicious sharks.

Polly spotted her friend Leo hiding behind an iceberg. Leo was a baby Leopard Seal that Polly had saved from a mean Orca whale several months ago. He loved swimming around and pretending to be a shark; he would use his flipper as a shark fin to trick the other animals. Polly waddled over to Leo, noticing the familiar smirk he had on his face. Then they both suddenly burst out belly laughing.

"Oh Leo, that was awesome! You really scared him this time," said Polly. They raised their flippers and jumped up as high as they could to give each other a *flipper-five*.

"Well, I've got to get home now. See you soon. Stay safe out there," said Leo as he slowly slipped off the edge of the iceberg and disappeared into the dark ocean.

Polly still sat there on the edge of the ice, shivering. She closed her eyes; she didn't want to remember that terrible day when she met Leo, but the memories came flooding back. His lifeless body was clenched tightly in the jaws of an orca whale. Polly shook with fear, remembering how scary that day was. She knew if she didn't save him, he would most certainly die. So, she saved him.

After Leo recovered from the attack, they became great friends. They shared their deepest secrets and most-treasured dreams with each other. As their friendship grew, they enjoyed scheming on the pranks they could use to give Malik a taste of his own medicine.

Polly smiled, thinking of her friendship with Leo. She slowly stood up and watched as darkness began to take over the once beautiful, sunny sky. Finally, she calmly turned and headed up the hill towards Malik.

"Polly, are you coming?" Malik said, over and over.

"Yes, I'm coming. Stop yelling at me!" Polly said with sharpness in her voice. Once she reached the top of the hill, Polly saw her brother racing toward the front door. As she got closer to home, she could smell the sweet aroma of Mama's homemade cod pie.

This had always been Polly's favorite dish for as long as she could remember. She wondered if there was a special reason Mama was making her favorite pie.

Did I forget Mama's birthday? Maybe we are having company.

Polly's mind was racing with thoughts of what it could be. Then all of a sudden, she stopped dead in her tracks.

"I know what it is!" she yelled with excitement. "We are all going on a trip!"

Her mind began racing! *Soft sand, warm sun, pretty beach umbrellas, and of course, her favorite pink floppy hat.* She felt the excitement building inside her. Her heart began pounding in her chest, faster and faster, with each step bringing her closer to home. Polly reached the front door and pushed it open so hard with her flipper, slamming it against the wall, making a loud banging noise.

"Polly dear, are you okay?" her Mama asked from the kitchen. Polly stood in the doorway and looked around the small white room. She noticed her father reclined in his chair with his feet up, flippers limp, and head slightly tilted down as he lay sound asleep, snoring as usual. By now, Malik was in his room playing his music and singing completely out of tune.

Polly quietly turned around and gently closed the door behind her. She didn't want to wake her father up. She slowly waddled her way into the kitchen with her head down, knowing what was to come.

"Hey Mama," Polly said sadly, as she watched her Mama making dinner.

"How was your day?" she asked her Mama.

"Oh, Polly, I had a wonderful day! All of my students are so excited about the new season. We talked for hours about all the new events coming up."

Her Mama turned around and wrapped Polly's face with both of her flippers and kissed her on the cheek. "Oh, I love you," Mama said as she scurried back over to the counter.

Polly sat down at the small wooden kitchen table Papa had made for them.

"We had such a good time!" Polly heard her Mama continue to talk about her day, but she wasn't really paying attention anymore. Instead, she was daydreaming about being surrounded by palm trees, sand, sun, and big white puffy clouds floating across the sky. But in her heart, she knew that was not going to happen.

"Are we going anywhere, Mama?"

"Polly, you interrupted me! No, of course not, sweetheart. I just wanted to make something special for your Papa for dinner. He's been working so hard teaching Malik and his classmates how to nurture their eggs."

Polly choked back the tears and said, "Oh, okay, Mama," as her voice trembled.

"What's the matter, Polly?"

"Nothing, Mama. I'm not hungry, and I don't feel very well. I'm going to my room."

Polly quickly waddled out of the kitchen and down the narrow hallway to her room. She didn't want her Mama to see her disappointment.

"Polly......POLLY!" her Mama said.

"I'll be okay. Don't worry, Mama. I just need some rest," Polly said as she entered her room. She immediately closed her door and sat down on her bed. She then tried to hold back the tears, but she couldn't stop them. The tears flowed. Polly laid down and covered her face with a pillow, trying not to sob too loudly.

After a few minutes, she finally sat up and just looked around at her beautiful room and smiled. Polly loved her room; her walls and ceiling were white, but she had covered them with vibrantly colored paintings of all the places she wanted to visit someday. Her bed was full of colorful feathers and a big, pink, furry blanket she had made. Her beach umbrella was leaning in the corner with her flipper flops and beach bag. Then, of course, there was her big pink, floppy hat that hung on a shell hook near her door.

Every night in her room, she would dream of traveling to faraway places. She dreamt of soaring high up into the sky while the sun was shining. She felt like she was floating on a cloud across the ocean.

What she couldn't imagine was staying in this cold, dark place, not even for another day.

Polly wasn't like everyone else; she wanted to do different things with her life.

She didn't want to live in the cold or swim in freezing water to search for food. Also, she didn't want her days filled with cooking or start a family yet. She didn't want any of those things.

Polly knew she was supposed to want these things, but she didn't want to do them! She felt like no one would understand her and wondered if something was wrong with her. She didn't like the long cold winters, ice, or snow. And, most of all, she didn't like the darkness; months and months of darkness.

Polly wiggled her way up under her pink blanket and wrapped it as tightly as she could around her. As she lay there, staring at the ceiling, she noticed there was something unusual underneath her flipper. Aggravated, Polly ripped off the covers and reached down by her flipper. There was a small book with a feather pen attached to the side. Polly noticed that there was a handwritten note pinned to the front. She picked up the small book, scooted her back against her wall, and placed it on her lap.

"I wonder who this is from?" Polly said as she gently opened it and began to read it out loud. The note was from her Mama.

My Dear Polly,

I was once your age... I yearned for something different and new, just like you. I wanted to see the world and dreamt about leaving this place all the time. I tried to leave many times, but I didn't. I couldn't find the courage to do it.

I have never told anyone how I felt, not even your Papa.

I always thought no one would understand, but you understand. I want you to follow your dreams. Follow them as far as they will take you. See the world, my baby girl.

All I want is for you to cherish every moment life has to offer. Life is too short not to do what makes you happy. Use this diary to tell your story. Write down your thoughts, your dreams—whatever you want to write about. Tell your story; whatever that story might hold is in your hands. I will always be here for you, no matter what you do in life, Polly. Always!

Love, Mama

Polly sat there, holding the small book tightly against her chest. She was surprised to learn that Mama knew how she felt. It made her happy to know that someone finally understood. She slowly opened the diary, pulled the feather pen from the side pocket, and starting writing.

Dear Diary,

Today was the last day of March, the day I always wished would never come. It brings so much darkness. I wish the sun were always out here all the time. I love feeling the warmth of the sun on my face. I want to be where there is lots of sunshine, but I'm scared. All I have ever known is being here. Everyone I love is here. What do I do? Do I stay? No. I have to go. I can do this! I need to be brave. I'm so tired. I think it's time for me to go to bed. Until next time. Good night my dear diary,

Polly

She laid her head down on her pillow. Her eyes were slowly closing, and she could feel her entire body going limp. She was so exhausted. Slowly, she drifted off to sleep. Soon, she would be dreaming of a place that was warm and sunny. A place far away from the cold. She would meet new friends and see beautiful things. This was a place she could be herself, and no one would judge her.

CHAPTER 2
A WHALE OF A DAY

"Polly! It's time to get your day started. You need to wake up and get ready for school. Get moving, young lady!" Mama said as she scurried down the hallway, headed for Malik's room next.

Polly sat up, stretched her flippers as far out as she could, and yawned.

"Okay, Mama. I'm up."

It was so warm and cozy under her fluffy blanket. Thoughts of the rest of her day outside in the cold and darkness made her sick to her stomach.

She slowly leaned over the side of the bed, reached down, picked up her diary, and tucked it in under the feathers. She wanted it hidden so no one would find it, not even Malik. It was hers and hers only!

Polly sat there, wrapped up in her blanket.

"I wish it wasn't a school day," she said as she poked her flippers out from under the cover.

"Burr! It's freezing in here," she added as she jumped up out of bed. She finally waddled her way to the kitchen for breakfast. Malik was already there, shoveling food in his mouth as if he'd never eaten before.

"Slow down, Malik, geez!" Polly said.

"You don't understand, Polly. Today is the day Dad will teach our class how to protect the eggs! We get to stand outside all week, day and night, practicing for the day when we have babies of our own to protect. If I don't hurry, I'll be late for class, and Dad will be furious with me!"

Polly glared in disbelief at his excitement for all of that. She looked away and rolled her eyes. She didn't realize her Mama was watching.

"Why are you rolling your eyes?" said Mama.

"Oh! I'm sorry. I was just joking around."

"Okay, Polly," her Mama said hesitantly.

Polly's Mama knew that something was wrong with her baby girl. She knew that Polly was not like everyone else. She wanted to help her but just didn't know how.

She was hoping that Polly had found the book last night with the note she had written. She wanted to believe that, in some way, it would help her little girl.

But she knew Polly was a lot like her when she was young; free-spirited, headstrong, and always looking for adventure. She had hopes that someday, Polly would settle down and have a family of her own, but she knew in her heart that would not make Polly happy. She stood there, deep in thought, staring out the window.

"Malik, you're going to be late!" Polly said as she looked over at her Mama, who was just quietly staring out the window.

"Are you okay, Mama?"

"Oh, yes, honey, I'm fine. After I get home from working at the school today, you and I will go out to our favorite spot and catch some fish, okay?" Mama said as she continued to look out the window, trying not to let Polly see her face.

"Okay," Polly said with a long sigh.

Finding food was the last thing Polly wanted to do.

"Now, don't you be late for school. I hope you have a good day," Mama said as she quickly grabbed her bag and headed out the door, trying not to look at Polly.

Polly just sat there at the table, staring at her breakfast. She didn't know how much longer she could stand doing the same routine over and over again. She was tired of eating the same meals every day.

She picked up her school bag and slid to the front door. As she stood up and opened the door, she stopped to look back at the beautiful home her parents had built.

She felt happy and sad at the same time. "Nothing's ever going to change," she said out loud, and like every other time, no one heard her.

Polly then rushed over to Patty's house. She always stopped to pick up Patty on her way to school. They had been best friends since they were born. Patty was her one true girlfriend. Polly always felt comfortable around her. She never had to hide her true self and always told Patty everything, well—almost everything. Patty was always a great listener. She was an Emperor Penguin too, just like Polly's Papa. She was very tall and quite big for her age. At school, Patty was always being picked on by the other penguins. They would call her names, but Polly never did. She was always there to help her friend, especially when the other penguins were being mean to her.

Patty was invariably kind to everyone. She was timid and ordinarily kept to herself. She had such a special bond with Polly, and they did everything together. You would never see one without the other. "Friends till the end," Polly would always say.

Polly knocked on Patty's door, but there was no answer. She knocked again, only harder this time. There was still no answer.

"Wanna go out to our favorite spot before school?" Polly yelled.

Finally, the door came flying open. "I'm so glad you're here," Patty said as she quickly shuffled right past Polly and out the front door with her feathers all ruffled up.

"Let's go!"

They took off as fast as they could; this always turned into a race. They would run, hop, and slide on the snow-dusted ice while laughing loudly, all the way to their favorite spot.

Polly reached the edge of the iceberg first. Just as she turned around to see where Patty was, she quickly jumped out of her way.

"Look out, Polly!" Patty said as she tried to use every ounce of might she had left, dragging her flippers frantically on the ice, hoping to stop herself.

Nevertheless, she wasn't able to stop and slid right off the bank and into the water.

"Oh my, this water is freezing, Polly! I just love cold water," Patty said as she jumped back up on the shore, shivering.

"Come on, Polly, let's swim on out a little further to the other iceberg before it gets any colder. Are you ready yet, Polly?"

Polly sat there with her head between her flippers, just wishing the sun would come out.

She knew that wasn't going to happen, not anytime soon. She couldn't understand why Patty thought swimming in this cold water was fun. Reluctantly, Polly stood up, poised to jump in.

"Yes, I'm ready, I guess."

"Race you!" Patty said as they both jumped in and swam as fast as they could in the icy waters.

They were both diving in and out of the water, laughing and giggling as they raced toward the massive iceberg, flippers flying everywhere.

"I win! You're too slow today, Polly," Patty said as she slumped over, gasping for air.

"Are you okay?" she added.

"Yeah… I'm fine," Polly said as she tried to shake the cold water off her silky black feathers.

"I'm just not happy here," she finally admitted.

"Why? Don't you like it here?" asked Patty with a curious look on her face.

"I just want to be somewhere warm. Someplace where the sun is always shining."

"Where would you go?"

"I don't know. I just don't want to be here," Polly answered as she sat there with her head down.

"Polly, you know we have to be in class soon, or we are going to be in a lot of trouble," Patty continued to ramble on about all the great things they were going to learn that day, but Polly just didn't care. She didn't want to be in that class.

That day at school was supposed to be a special outing. It would be their first official fishing trip. Polly didn't need that class as she had been fishing with her Mama for months. She sat there with her head up, flippers out to the side, daydreaming.

"Polly," Patty said. "POLLY! Snap out of it. I've got something to tell you. I think I've finally met *the one*. He's so handsome and tall. Oh, Polly, I think I'm in love."

Polly spun around so quickly that she knocked Patty's book bag right out of her flipper.

"What?" Polly said. "When did this happen?"

"Polly, he came over last night and met my parents. They loved him. I can't wait for you to meet him too."

Polly just stood there, frozen. She didn't know what to say. Having a boyfriend or even a family was not what Polly wanted at all, or at least, not anytime soon.

"Why didn't you tell me?"

"I don't know. It happened so suddenly. I tried to tell you the other day, but I just couldn't."

"I'm happy for you, Patty. I really am. Anyway, we should probably get going before we are late for school."

Polly turned away from the water and tried not to cry. She wasn't jealous of her friend. She just didn't want the same things as Patty.

She knew deep down in her heart that Patty would always stay here. She knew she would start a family someday soon.

"Maybe someday you can meet him, Polly," Patty said with excitement as she sat on the edge of the iceberg with her flippers splashing up and down.

"Oh, Polly, look, it's Wilber and Willamina!"

Wilber and Willamina were huge, beautiful, gentle Orca Whales. Much like her Mama and her Papa, they were always together. They seemed so happy.

Polly longed for what they had. They were free and traveled hundreds of miles together, all while jumping in and out of the water. The thing Polly loved most about them was the magical songs they sang as they swam and breached out of the water.

Polly met Wilber and Willamina on a warm and sunny afternoon. She had been frolicking around in the water, jumping in and out, and spinning high in the air, just enjoying the warm sunshine.

Then suddenly she noticed a huge whale out of the corner of her eye.

The whale came flying out of the water, flipping onto its back, and was set to land directly on top of Polly.

Polly tried to get out of the way as fast as she could, but the whale's weight hitting the water forced her down towards the bottom of the ocean, knocking the wind out of her.

Polly frantically tried to catch her breath; she was dizzy and disoriented and couldn't tell which way was up. She tried not to panic, but she could feel her life slipping away. Everything started going dark. She couldn't muster up any energy to fight any longer. She just knew this was going to be the end. She closed her eyes, and her body went limp.

Suddenly, a whale swooped down from somewhere in the dark waters and cradled Polly's limp body under her flipper. The whale swam as close as she could get to the iceberg. She laid Polly down gently and slowly rubbed her belly, hoping that Polly would wake up.

In that moment, another whale noticed what was going on and made its way to help. As he approached Polly, he made a loud, screeching noise, which seemed to shake everything surrounding them. Then he slammed a flipper down onto the ice. Polly jumped up to her feet and coughed up all the water she had inhaled.

She stood there in awe, staring at these two humongous whales. She didn't know whether to run or stand completely still, hoping that they wouldn't see her.

"Oh my, you poor little thing. Are you okay?" said the whale that pulled Polly from the bottom of the ocean.

"Yes, I am," Polly said, still shaking some.

"My name is Willamina, and this is my husband, Wilber."

"I'm Polly."

"Well, Polly, my dear, I'm so sorry that I hit you. I hope you will be okay."

"I'll be fine," Polly said, standing there with her mouth wide open in amazement.

"You aren't going to eat me, are you?" she added.

Wilber began to snort and flipped over backward, then jumped and slid up onto the iceberg. They were nose to nose. Polly could feel the warm air from his nose like a gust of wind every time he took a breath. She had never been this close to a whale, ever.

"Not all Orcas are bad, Polly, and besides, I'm not hungry right now," he said as he chuckled and slid down off the ice and under the water.

Polly didn't know whether to laugh or cry.

"Oh, Polly, he's just kidding. Would you like to take a ride on my back across this beautiful ocean?"

"Oh yes, I would love that, I think…" Polly said nervously.

"Don't be scared, dear. Hop on!"

Polly hesitantly jumped onto Willamina's back. She then held on tightly to her fin as they took off out into the ocean. Polly soon developed a strong trust with them. The couple would come back every summer and take Polly for rides all over the vast ocean.

They would take her to all kinds of pretty places she had never seen before, and she was also certain if she ever needed help, they would be there for her.

"Polly! Stop daydreaming and pay attention. Are you watching? Look, they're having so much fun jumping and splashing." said Patty.

Polly turned and looked at Wilber and Willamina with a tear running down her rosy cheek feathers. She didn't want Patty to see her crying.

"Yes, I'm watching," said Polly, wiping her tears off her face. She was happy for Wilber and Willamina, but she knew it was time for them to head towards warmer waters. They had to meet up with family. Polly missed them so much every time they left.

Slowly, Willamina slid herself up onto the ice right between Polly and Patty.

"Oh, Polly," said Willamina. "How are you doing, sweetheart?"

Polly lifted her head, trying not to appear troubled.

"Polly, my dear, this shall also pass, just as it does every year. You know we always come back here to our favorite place. Time will go by so quickly, and when your school is out, Wilber and I will be here. We will have so much to tell you."

"I know," said Polly.

"I want you to have a wonderful trip, but I will miss you both so much," Polly said as she sat, almost frozen on the ice with Patty.

Wilber and Willamina took off, jumping high above the moonlit water, singing their beautiful songs.

"See you soon, girls," Willamina called back.

Polly and Patty jumped up and down, yelling with excitement. They were so happy to see them dancing up and over the water.

"Okay, Polly, it's time to get to school. We have to head back now, or we are going to be late," said Patty.

Polly was shivering. Her fins were cold, but she turned, leaped as high as she could, and dove deep down into the water.

"Hey! Wait for me!" Patty yelled.

They both swam as fast as they could towards the shore. They were jumping over each other, flipping all around, and having a blast.

"Seriously, we've had enough fun! Let's get to school," Patty said as they reached the shore.

Polly was not paying any attention to Patty. She was laughing and rolling around all over the place.

Patty kept trying to get Polly's attention. She finally screamed as loud as she could.

"STOP IT!" Patty sternly said.

Polly stopped and stood there, shocked.

"I'm sorry," Polly said with a sigh.

"We were having so much fun. I forgot about school. Let's get going."

They dropped down onto their bellies and scurried off towards the school.

CHAPTER 3
PETREL ISLAND

Most days after school, Patty and Polly would meet up with Stormy, their crazy Petrel bird friend. The three would then head off to a remote area to catch some krill, talk about their day, and most importantly, laugh.

"We haven't seen Stormy in a couple of days. Come on, let's go out to Petrel Island and see if we can find him. I hope he's okay," said Polly.

"Petrel Island?" said Patty hesitantly.

"That place is insane, Polly. There are thousands of birds squawking and flying everywhere.

We will never find him there. Besides, every time I go there, some stupid bird poops on me. It's just plain nasty!"

Polly fell over backward, laughing. She was laughing so hard that she could barely catch her breath.

"That's not funny, Polly! Stop laughing at me!"

"I'm sorry, maybe you need to learn to duck under the water a little faster," Polly said as she continued to laugh so hard; her belly was hurting.

"Okay, okay—seriously Patty, we have to try. What if he is hurt?"

"Oh, alright. But if I get pooped on again, I'm never going back there. Ever!"

Polly was still giggling as she said, "Let's get going. Come on, walk like this, Patty."

Polly, acting silly, began to waddle back and forth like a duck towards the water.

"You're so silly Polly. Okay, I'm coming."

Patty took off, mimicking Polly as they slid off into the water and headed towards Petrel Island. They jumped in and out, crisscrossing in mid-air, twirling around, and seeing who could make the biggest splash. Soon, they were at Petrel Island. They looked up from out of the water and slid up onto the ice.

"Remember to duck, Patty," Polly said with a slight snicker in her voice.

"Not funny, Polly."

Without going up onto the island, the girls swam all around it, looking for Stormy. Stormy was nowhere to be found. They both called for him over and over. Then suddenly, they could hear Stormy yelling back to them from somewhere in the middle of this hugely overcrowded colony.

"Hang on, girls! I'm coming!"

Stormy was stuck in the middle of this huge sea of birds. He struggled to work his way out of the pack. Finally, he was able to muscle his way through. He jumped up as high as he could and swirled around high above the ice. He then swooped down with his wings tucked tight to his body. He flew right over Polly and Patty, just missing the tops of their heads. They both ducked quickly.

"Almost gotcha! Oh, no!" he said as he plummeted towards the ice and started sliding uncontrollably. He fought with every ounce of might he could muster up to stop, but his feet were quickly whipped right out from under him. He crashed head first into a massive iceberg

"HELP! Polly, help me!" he yelled.

Ice and snow fell all around him, and the girls couldn't help but laugh. They laughed so hard they could barely hear Stormy.

"That wasn't funny," Stormy said.

"I'm sorry," said Patty.

Stormy slowly got up and shook off all the ice that landed on top of him—shivering from the cold.

"Where are my glasses? I can't see a thing. Polly, help me!" Stormy said as he wandered around aimlessly, using his wings to frantically search the ice for them.

"Hang on, silly. I found them," Polly said as she handed them to him.

Stormy grabbed them with his wings and placed them upside down on his nose.

"Everything looks weird. I'm getting dizzy," he said faintly.

Polly leaned over, took his glasses off, and turned them right side up.

"Better?" Polly said as she tried not to laugh.

"Yes, thank you very much," Stormy said as he strutted around with his chest poked out and wings all perked up. "So, how are my two favorite girls doing today?"

"Oh, pretty good," said Patty. "At least I didn't get pooped on today."

"Okay," Polly said, still giggling over the poop talk.

"On a serious note," Polly continued, "I need to talk to both of you. It's really important,"

"Let's head out to our favorite spot!" Patty swiftly responded.

The three of them took off. They all headed out to their favorite place, Big Rock.

As expected, it was always a race to see who would get their first. Surprisingly, Stormy won this time.

"Wow, Stormy! You were flying fast," Polly said.

"Yeah, I was. So, what's up? You seem awfully distracted today," Stormy said as he quickly adjusted his glasses and positioned his wings on his hips.

He stretched his long neck out toward Polly, intently waiting on her reply.

"Guys, I've decided I'm going on an adventure," Polly softly said.

Stormy and Patty just stood there, looking at each other. They were completely dumbfounded by what they had just heard.

"What does that mean, Polly?" said Patty.

"I've decided I'm not staying here in this place anymore. I'm going to travel the world."

There was complete silence. All that could be heard was the waves breaking in the distance.

"Well... Does anyone want to go with me?"

Patty stood there, looking at Polly. She was doing everything she could to stop tears from running down her face.

"Polly, I can't leave here. Everything I have ever known is here. Why would you want to leave?"

"You know how much I don't like it here. I just want to be happy; see new things and meet new people. I want to do it all!"

Stormy hadn't said a word. He observed silently as the girls talked. He was sad to hear that his friend would leave, but deep down in his heart, he knew Polly wasn't meant to stay there. He had heard all about her big dreams; she always talked about all the beautiful places she would love to visit someday. He wasn't surprised at all.

Stormy noticed there was this awkward silence between the girls.

"I think it's a great idea. Where will you go first?" asked Stormy, breaking the silence.

Polly looked over at Patty. She could see that she was obviously upset and about to cry.

"Not now, Stormy," Polly said in a shaking tone. "Are you okay, Patty?"

Patty was upset. She quickly turned around and started heading towards the edge of the water. She paused for a moment and looked back at Polly.

"Bye, guys. I've got to go. I'm going to be late for dinner," Patty said as she hurriedly jumped into the water and disappeared into the darkness. Before Polly could even say goodbye, Patty was gone.

"Stormy, I know Patty is upset. What do I do?" Polly asked as her voice seemed to crack.

"Polly, you have to do what makes you happy. Patty will be fine. She's just going to miss you. Just talk to her."

"So, when are you going on your adventure?"

"Well, earlier today, I slipped a note to Leo. He will give it to Willamina, hoping that she will be able to find Abby and Alvin. Do you remember them? They are those big Albatross birds that are always way down by the cove. I want to see if they will fly me somewhere."

"Oh wow, Polly! You're going to fly with Abby and Alvin across hundreds of miles of ocean. Are you crazy?" Stormy said as he started running around in circles.

"I would never fly that far over the ocean! Anyone that flies that far over the ocean is crazy! You have to be nuts to do that," he said while still running around in circles.

Polly knew that Stormy always acted this way whenever he was nervous or upset. She had to stop him before he got hurt.

"Stop!" Polly said.

Stormy abruptly stopped right in his tracks, almost like he was standing to attention in school.

"Stormy, stop that. It's going to be okay. Hopefully, I will get to talk to Abby and Alvin tomorrow about it. I hope they will help me."

"You are seriously crazy. Cute, but crazy. Those huge birds are so scary."

"Stormy, no they're not."

Polly actually didn't know them very well, but they seemed nice. They were a quiet pair and stayed pretty much to themselves.

Polly always admired their beauty and grace when they flew. They used their seemingly vast wingspan to ride the ocean winds. At times, they would glide for hours without stopping. Polly stood there, daydreaming about riding along with them, just floating up in the sky with the clouds.

"Polly! I'll go with you," said Stormy.

Polly turned around quickly, bent over, looked right into Stormy's eyes, and said, "Will you?"

"I...I...I think so. Polly, I have to tell you something." Stormy leaned in and whispered, "I'm a little scared to fly."

Polly fell over backward, holding her stomach as she laughed hard.

"Polly, that's not funny!"

"You're a bird. You have to admit it. It's a little funny."

"Never mind, I've got to get back to the colony. See you later," Stormy said as he turned around and began walking with his head down towards his home.

"Wait, I'm sorry. I didn't know you were really afraid to fly."

"Well, technically, I'm not afraid to fly. I'm afraid of heights, so I just fly low."

Polly stood there, doing everything she could to stop herself from bursting into laughter. There was dead silence.

"Well, can I go with you?"

Polly looked at him. She was not sure if or how this was going to work. She knew she could really use a friend, and it was obvious that Patty would never go.

"Of course, you can come with me," she said.

Polly ran over and wrapped her flippers around Stormy. "I'm so excited! Gotta go, Stormy." Polly quickly turned and slid off the edge into the water.

"I'll see you tomorrow after I talk to Abby and Alvin," she added, and Stormy nodded in agreement.

"See you soon, Polly!" Stormy said as he flew off and headed towards his colony.

All the way home, Polly was jumping and singing. She was overjoyed with the thought of someone else sharing this journey with her. Finally, someone understood.

CHAPTER 4
MIGHTY MIDGE

"Polly! Wake up! It's time for school," said Malik.

He yelled for her to wake up over and over.

"I'm awake. Stop yelling at me. It's Saturday."

Polly sat up, wrapped in her pink fuzzy blanket.
She sat there thinking about her day.

"Today's the day," she said while jumping out of
bed with a big smile on her face. She was so excited not
to be in school and hoped she would hear from Abby and
Alvin today.

She then rushed past Malik as he was lollygagging in the hallway and slid straight for the front door.

"See you later!" Polly happily shouted.

"Bye, have fun," said Malik with a curious look on his face. He knew Polly was up to something but had no idea what it could be.

Polly was so excited to meet up with Leo. She slid as fast as she could to the meeting spot. When she finally got to the edge of the iceberg, Leo was nowhere to be found.

"Leo said he would be here early. Did I miss him already?" she said out loud.

She was determined to wait. She sat there hoping and wishing he would come jumping up onto the iceberg with good news. It seemed like hours had gone by, and there was still no Leo. Polly was getting cold and shivering already.

I guess he isn't coming. Maybe he couldn't find Willamina. Maybe they couldn't find Abby and Alvin, she thought.

Abby and Alvin were beautiful birds but very reclusive, after all. Polly wanted to believe that he could find them and give them the note, but she had been waiting there for quite some time.

There was still no sign of them. Polly then dropped her head down and wrapped her flippers tightly around her body to try to stay warm. After waiting almost the entire day, she finally decided it was time to head back home.

She was so cold, and she knew she would get in trouble if she was out too late. Just as Polly started to turn around and leave, she heard Leo's voice.

"Polly! Polly!" Leo yelled.

She could feel the excitement building up in her chest. Leo hopped up onto the ice and slid right up to her.

"Where have you been?" Polly asked.

"I'm so sorry. I spent all night with Willamina trying to find Abby and Alvin for you."

Polly's heart began to race.

"And?" she asked.

"They're coming, Polly. They are coming."

Polly couldn't believe this was all happening. She was at a loss for words. She sat there staring up at the moonlit sky, watching and waiting for Abby and Alvin to fly over at any moment. She had only seen them fly a few times. Their wingspan was epic and elegant. They literally floated across the breeze over the ocean.

"Is everything okay, Polly?"

"Oh, Leo, I'm so grateful that you were able to find them."

"Well, don't thank me! Smoosh was the one that found them."

"Smoosh?!" Polly said in disbelief.

Polly did not like Smoosh. He was a mean little bird that was always stealing eggs from the other penguins.

"I can't believe you asked Smoosh to help."

"Polly, I know you don't like him, but he's my friend, and I couldn't have done it without him. Please, give him a chance."

Smoosh was hiding behind Leo, shaking with fear.

He was hoping Polly wouldn't, well—smoosh him.

Smoosh and Leo had been friends for a really long time. He was always sitting on top of Leo everywhere he went. Many times, he would just stand with his head up tall and beak open. His wings were always stretched out like he was about to take flight, and he always seemed like he was up to something. Polly could never quite figure him out.

"Hey, Polly," said Smoosh. "Abby and Alvin will be here soon."

Polly just glared at him. She couldn't believe he would help her after everything he had done, torturing her colony. Polly remembered her Papa chasing him several times to keep him away from their eggs.

"I…I'm really sorry for all the terrible things I've done. Truly, I mean it. Leo has told me so much about you."

Polly always had a hard time staying mad at anyone.

She was willing to give Smoosh another chance—after all, he had helped find Abby and Alvin. She ran over to him, snatched him out from behind Leo, and wrapped him up with both her flippers.

She then squeezed him as tight as she could, leaned over, and whispered in his ear, "Thank you, Smoosh. Maybe you're not so bad after all, but I better never find you anywhere near my colony or touching another one of our eggs again. You got that?"

Smoosh started shaking all over.

"Okay, Polly. I promise," he said as he tried to slideout from under Polly's flippers. Polly just turned and winked at Leo.

"That was funny," said Leo.

The three of them sat there in silence, waiting on Abby and Alvin.

"Are you sure they are coming, Leo?" asked Polly.

"I promise. They said they'd be here," said Smoosh, still hiding behind Leo.

"Look," said Leo. "I see them!"

Polly looked up at the dark sky. They looked so small from a distance, but Polly knew they weren't small at all. They all stood there, staring up at the sky.

They watched as Abby and Alvin floated through the sky side by side, swooping down across the water, in and out of the moonlight.

It was so beautiful and graceful, Polly thought.

Finally, they landed so gently next to Polly. She was in awe of how beautiful they were. They all were.

"So, you must be Polly," said Abby.

Polly just stood there with her mouth open, staring at Abby and Alvin. She couldn't believe that they were there.

"Aren't you going to talk to Alvin or Abby?" Leo said as he nudged Polly closer to them.

"Oh! Yes. Hi, I'm Polly the penguin!"

"Well, hello, Polly the penguin. So, what exactly can we do for you?" asked Alvin.

"I… I… I need your help."

"Help? How can we help you, Polly?" Abby asked.

"I want to fly...away...from here," she said. She was so nervous and could hardly get the words out.

"Okay, you do realize that penguins can't fly," said Abby, chuckling.

Polly knew she had to get this right. She had to ask for their help, and this was her only hope of getting away from here.

"Can you fly me to Australia?" Polly asked.

Abby and Alvin just looked at each other. They didn't know what to say.

"You want us to fly you to Australia?" asked Alvin.

"Yes. Me and my friend, Stormy," Polly nervously said.

Abby and Alvin turned away from the group and muttered to each other. Leo, Polly, and Smoosh waited in anticipation.

"Okay! We will do it," said Abby. "We are leaving in the morning. Can you both be ready by then?"

"Oh, yes! Yes, we can. I don't know how to thank you. I'm so excited!"

Abby leaned over and put her wing around Polly.

"Polly, Australia is beautiful. I love it there. You and your friend, Stormy, will love it there too. We go there every year."

Polly looked on, intrigued, hanging on to their every word. She had no idea how far Australia was, and she didn't care. It was going to be a fantastic trip.

"Well, time for us to go catch dinner, Alvin. You ready, dear?"

"Yes, I'm ready."

Alvin turned and looked intently at Polly and Stormy.

"We leave early! It's a long flight. I hope you're both ready!" Alvin said as he swooped off the iceberg and flew up into the moonlight.

"See you two tomorrow," Abby said as she slowly floated off into the sky, side by side with Alvin.

"You did it, Polly! You're leaving this place," Leo excitedly said.

Polly was elated. "I need to get packing! What do I take, Leo?" she asked.

"Well, I'm not sure, but I would pack light. Australia is far, far away."

"Guys, I don't know how to thank you for helping me."

"Just come back someday and tell us all about your incredible journey. I can't wait to hear all about it," Leo said as he jumped into the water, splashing everyone.

"Don't forget about us, Polly," said Smoosh as he hopped on Leo's back.

"Smoosh, will you tell Stormy for me?" Polly asked.

"Yes, yes I will," Smoosh said with a smile.

Polly took off for home and waved back at the two of them. There were so many things racing through her mind. She was so excited. Finally, she was going to fulfill her dreams.

Soon, her excitement turned to uncertainty. Reality was setting in, and she became overwhelmed with doubt. She stopped at the top of the hill by her house.

"What am I going to tell Mama and Papa? What about Malik? How do I tell Patty?" Her head was spinning. *"Do I tell them at all or just leave them a note?"*

Her heart sank. She slowly waddled over to her house. She then leaned her back against the door and slid down. Out of confusion, she just sat there in the cold.

"What do I do?" she said out loud.

"Well, if it was me, I wouldn't tell them," said a tiny voice.

Polly looked all around, trying to figure out where the voice was coming from.

"Who's out there?"

"It's me, Midge. Down here, on your flipper."

"Midge, I haven't seen you in forever!"

"Probably because I spend most of my time frozen," he said, then laughed.

"Yes, yes, you do," Polly chuckled.

"So, I hear you're leaving this place tomorrow."

"How did you know?" Polly asked.

Midge was laughing so hard that he fell off the feather he was clinging to and landed upside down on the ground. Polly gently picked Midge up and set him on her lap.

"Midge, you were with me all day?"

"Sorry, I couldn't help myself. I get so bored here, and it seemed like you were heading out for some fun. So—I jumped up, grabbed a feather, and held on for dear life. It was a crazy day too, wow!"

Polly was not happy with Midge.

"Really, Midge?" she asked.

Polly knew there wasn't much for Midge to do there. In fact, he really did spend nine months of his life frozen.

He only got to enjoy life for the short three months a year that the sun was out. She also knew he didn't have any friends. There were no other insects that could live in the cold weather of Antarctica. So, reluctantly she would take him with her whenever she could.

Midge was a tiny ant, but mighty for his size. One time, Polly saw Midge move a rock a hundred times his size from the top of the hill to the front door.

She couldn't believe it. Polly always worried that she would squash him, but he was really quick to get out of the way.

Apparently, he was used to getting stepped on. Polly started laughing to herself.

"What's so funny, Polly?"

"Oh, nothing. So, what do I do? Should I tell anyone or just leave?"

"If it were me, I'd just leave. But you have a family that loves you, Polly. I've been around your family enough to know that you should tell them the truth. I think you know that's what you have to do."

"Really? I haven't said anything to anyone yet."

"You may not have to say anything, Polly. I'm pretty sure they can tell something is up. It's written all over your face."

"I'm going to miss everyone so much, but I need to do this Midge."

"I know, but think of how much more fun it will be to have your family's support. They'll be worried sick if you leave without telling them," Midge said, staring up at Polly.

Polly nodded in agreement.

"You're right. I'm going to go talk to Mama. I'll see you later," she said as she carefully placed Midge down on his favorite rock.

"Take care of yourself, Midge," she added.

"Bye, Polly, good luck."

Polly smiled and watched as Midge slowly crawled under his rock.

She turned and quietly opened the door, hoping she would go unnoticed.

As she softly waddled across the living room, she stopped right in the middle of her house, memorizing every inch of her home as she stood there. She thought back on all the great things that had happened there. She was going to miss this place, her friends, and mostly, her family. Even still, she knew in her heart that she had to go.

Mama walked into the room and noticed Polly just standing there by herself.

"Sweetheart, what are you doing?"

"Mama, can we talk? Alone?"

"Of course, sweetheart. Let's go into the kitchen. Your Papa will be late tonight, and Malik is on his class field trip. Let me make us some seaweed tea, and we'll talk."

Polly sat down at the table, trying desperately to hold back her tears.

"Here, drink this. It will warm you right up," Mama said.

Mama was always so caring and understanding to everyone.

"Mama…"

"I know what you're going to say, sweetheart."

Polly looked right at her Mama as her tears began flowing down her face.

"How do you know?"

"Polly, dear, I've known for a long time that being here is not what you want for your life. As a young girl, I was just like you, Polly. I also wanted to travel and see the world. I used to tell your grandmother that all the time, and of course, she didn't want to hear any of it," Mama said, with a hint of sorrow in her voice.

"Polly, I truly want you to be happy."

Polly just sat there in awe, listening intently, hanging onto every word. Mama continued to talk about all the things she wished she could have done; places she wanted to see. Polly was amazed. Mama leaned over, wrapped her flippers around her, and hugged her.

"I will always love you, no matter what you choose to do. Always remember that," Mama softly said.

Polly couldn't hold in it any longer. She finally told her Mama all about her new adventure. To her surprise, Mama was so excited for her.

They sat there together; drank their tea while talking and laughing about everything for hours. Polly loved spending time alone with her Mama. She knew she was going to miss her so much.

They hugged each other tightly as Mama whispered gently in her ear, "I love you my sweet baby girl."

"Now, Polly, you need to go get your things packed. Tomorrow is your big day."

Polly jumped up and waddled as fast as she could towards her room.

"I love you too, Mama! Oh, one more thing," she said as she stood in the hallway.

"What is it, Polly?" Mama said from the kitchen.

"What about Papa and Malik? I can't forget about Patty either!" she said.

All at once, as she entered her room, she felt a mixture of overwhelming emotions. With her shoulders slumped and her head down, she slowly sat down on her bed. Mama followed Polly to her room and sat next to her. She then wrapped her flipper around her beautiful daughter and said, "Sweetheart, everything is going to be okay."

"Mama, I'm scared," Polly said in a faint tone.

Mama leaned forward and gently pulled Polly's face close to hers.

"You are a beautiful young lady. I have taught you well. You are intelligent, strong, and courageous. I have no doubt you will be just fine, my darling. Go! Go, fulfill your dreams. You can do this."

Mama slowly hopped off the bed and waddled towards Polly's door. All at once, she stopped, turned around, and smiled at her daughter.

"Polly, don't you worry. I will talk to Papa and Malik."

Mama started back down the hallway which led to the kitchen. Then suddenly, she stopped, realizing that she had not mentioned Patty.

"Oh, by the way, don't you worry about Patty. She knows, Polly!"

"Does she?" Polly yelled back with excitement.

"Yes, yes she does," Mama said with a chuckle.

"She will be there when you leave, Polly. I promise."

Polly couldn't believe it! How exciting that her best friend would be there for her.

"Will you be there, Mama?" she asked.

"Of course, darling. I wouldn't miss it," Mama said as she smiled to herself.

Polly closed her door gently and sat down on her bed. She grabbed her big pink blanket and just fell back onto all the feathers.

"I can't believe it. I'm really leaving!"

Mama could hear Polly packing in her bedroom. Polly talked, sang, and laughed to herself while trying to decide what she would take with her. Her Mama's heart was filled with joy knowing Polly would be happy.

She could hear the excitement in her voice. Mama just sat quietly at the table, sipping her tea and listening to her daughter.

Polly finally finished packing. She sat down on her bed and was so exhausted from the day that she could barely keep her eyes open.

"Oh no, I almost forgot to pack my new diary."

She reached down under the feathers on her bed and pulled it out. She held it in her hands, just staring at it for a while. Then she pulled the pen out and opened the book.

Dear Diary,

Tonight is my last night here for a long time. I'm so excited to start this new chapter in my life. I can't believe that Abby and Alvin will be flying Stormy and me all the way to Australia! I'm so excited! I bet Stormy is too. They are such huge, beautiful birds. They seem so sweet and caring. I wouldn't have been able to do this if it wasn't for Leo and Smoosh. Oh, and I can't forget Wilber and Willamina. How can I ever repay them for their kindness? I'm so tired. I hope I sleep tonight.

Oh, Diary, I'm so thankful for my family. Mama seems so happy for me. I wish she could come with me, but I know she has to stay here for Papa and Malik. I will write to her, I promise. Well, I better get to sleep. It's getting late, and I've got to be up early.

Polly

Polly slowly slipped down under her feather blanket. She then folded her book up and placed it in her backpack. Soon she would be dreaming of her new adventure.

CHAPTER 5
COMING TO AN ICEBERG NEAR YOU

"Polly, time to wake up," Mama said.

Polly sat straight up and stretched her flippers as far out as she could.

"I'm so excited, Mama!"

"Well, you need to get all your things together. I've got breakfast ready for you," Mama said and scurried off back to the kitchen.

Polly jumped out of bed and picked up her backpack.

As she hurried out of the room, she stopped at the door and turned back around to look, just one more time.

She smiled as she looked at all her drawings on the ceilings and walls.

"Come on, dear. We can't be late."

Polly slowly and quietly closed her door so she wouldn't wake up Papa and headed to the kitchen. Much to Polly's surprise, her Papa was already at the table, having his morning coffee.

"Good morning, young lady," Papa said.

"Oh! Good morning, Papa," Polly responded as she looked over at her Mama with her eyes wide. She was stunned that her Papa was sitting there.

"It's okay Polly. Your Papa knows. Now sit down with us, and let's have some breakfast before you go."

Mama placed each breakfast plate neatly in front of them.

"Prayers, papa?" Mama said in her gentle, calm voice.

Papa said the morning prayers, and they all sat silently to enjoy their meal. Polly was eating so fast that she started choking on her food.

"Polly, slow down dear, we have plenty of time."

When everyone was finished, Polly helped her Mama clean up the kitchen.

"Where's Malik, Mama?"

"Polly, remember? He's on his field trip from school."

"So, he doesn't know, right?"

"No, Polly, he doesn't. I will talk to him later this week when he gets home. Now let's get your things and go pick up Patty on our way, okay?"

Polly was filled with so much excitement, yet her heart was breaking. She would miss everyone so much. She slowly grabbed her backpack and headed towards the door.

"Polly," her Papa said from his easy chair. "I love you. Please be careful and be sure to write to us to let us know how you are doing."

Polly nodded her head in response. Then tears overwhelmed her, and she ran over to her father's chair. She jumped up on his lap and laid her head on his shoulder. Papa wrapped his flippers tightly around his beautiful daughter, just like he would always do.

"You will be fine. You have grown into an amazing young woman. Just remember, you always have a home to come back to, and you will always be my little princess."

Polly just smiled and softly kissed her Papa on the cheek.

"Love you too, Papa."

Polly hopped up from his lap.

"I'm ready to go Mama," she said.

Mama and Polly took off on their bellies towards Patty's house, sliding side by side. Polly was enjoying the quiet time of the early morning hours. Everything was so still and calm.

It was so surreal, something she would surely miss. All you could hear was her and Mama sliding on the ice guided by the moonlight. Soon, they were at Patty's.

"Patty, are you ready to go?" Polly loudly said as she knocked on her door.

Patty opened up the door with a perplexed look on her face.

"Are you okay, Polly?" Patty asked.

"Yes, I think so. Are you still going to be my friend, Patty?"

"Of course, I will! I'm going to miss you so much, but I will always be your friend. Friends till the end, remember?" They hugged each other tightly.

"Girls, we have to go before Abby and Alvin leave without Polly," said Mama.

The three then took off on their bellies and slid across the ice. Both girls followed Polly's Mama up and over each snow pile. They were laughing and giggling like they always did. Finally, they arrived where they would all meet. Polly could see Leo sitting on the edge of the iceberg.

"Leo, you're here," said Polly.

"Of course, I am."

Polly's Mama was taken aback by the sight of Leo.

"Polly, who is that?"

"Oh, it's okay, Mama. This is my friend, Leo. He won't hurt you; I promise."

Polly's Mama watched as they all gave each other rump bumps, flipper-fives, and pushed each other off into the water. They were having so much fun.

"Well, Leo, where are Abby and Alvin?" Polly politely asked.

"They should be here any minute now."

The anticipation was growing. She was nervous, sad, and excited, all at the same time.

"I want you to have the time of your life," Mama said to Polly. "I will miss you more than you will ever know."

"I will miss you too," said Patty. "Please send us pictures and letters."

"But I don't have any way to take pictures."

"Yes, you do! This is my present for you," Patty said as she handed Polly the camera that she got for her birthday last month.

"Patty, I can't take that. That was your birthday present."

"Please take some beautiful pictures and send them back to me."

"Oh, Patty, I don't know what to say. Thank you so much."

"Polly! Look, here they come," Leo yelled.

The four just stood there and watched as Abby and Alvin flew over their heads. They were all in awe of their size and beauty. Abby landed first, then Alvin.

"Polly, darling, are you ready to go?" said Abby.

"Yes, I am!" Polly hesitantly said as she turned to look at her Mama.

Abby could tell Polly's Mama was apprehensive about her daughter leaving with strangers. She slowly walked over to Polly's Mama and said, "Hello, I'm Abby, and this is my husband, Alvin."

Polly's Mama was stunned by how big they were. Their wingspan was far-reaching.

"Wow, you're beautiful," said Mama. "Please take good care of my baby girl."

"Oh, no worries, we will get her safely to Australia in a couple of days," said Alvin.

Polly turned around and hugged her Mama one more time.

"I will be careful, Mama. Please don't worry. Patty, I will send you lots of pictures. Leo, please take care and be safe. I will miss you all dearly."

"Oh, no, wait, I almost forgot," said Polly. "Where's Stormy?"

"Stormy's going with you?" Patty said.

"He said he was. Maybe he changed his mind."

Polly was a little disappointed that Stormy wasn't there, but she needed to go.

Abby and Alvin were waiting for her. So, with the help of Leo, she hopped up on Alvin's back.

"Well, time for us to get started on this wonderful journey! Are you ready Polly dear?" said Abby.

"WAIT!" Stormy screeched. "I'm coming in hot!"

Everyone stopped what they were doing. They turned around and looked up. Stormy was flying like a wobbly Frisbee. He had one wing on his glasses and the other on his backpack.

"Oh, this isn't going to be good," Polly said nervously.

Stormy was flying in way too fast, and his weight was shifting from side to side.

"Duck!" he yelled as he flipped over and hit the ice, beak first. His entire head was stuck in the ice, and only his wings and feet were sticking up.

Patty quickly ran over to check on Stormy.

"Are you okay?" she asked.

Polly jumped off Alvin's back and ran over to help Stormy too. She then looked over at Patty, and both were trying not to laugh.

"Patty, help me pull him out."

Polly and Patty pulled and pulled while Stormy was pushing with everything he had. Finally, they yanked on him so hard, he popped out of the hole. He flipped over backward and slid right into Alvin.

"Oops! I'm sorry, sir," said Stormy.

Alvin just laughed and said, "Are you okay, little buddy?"

Everyone started to giggle as Stormy got up and brushed himself off, looking for his glasses and backpack.

"I can't find my backpack," Stormy said.

"Well, maybe these glasses will help," Polly said as she held his glasses high over his head.

Stormy kept trying to jump up and get them.

"Stop it! That's not funny."

"Oh, yes, it is," Polly said as she giggled.

"Here's your backpack, Stormy," Patty said with a slight smirk.

"Okay, is everybody ready now?" asked Alvin.

Polly hopped back up on Alvin's back and wrapped her flippers tightly around his neck. Stormy flew up onto Abby's back. Abby then swooped down off the iceberg and spun upward toward the moonlight. Alvin, on the other hand, stood still for just a few moments.

"Polly, are you ready?" he asked.

"Yes, I am! Bye, everyone!" Polly excitedly replied.

"Polly! Friends till the end, always," Patty cheered.

"Flipper-Five, Polly," Leo yelled.

"We all love you! Be safe, my baby girl," Mama said as she watched her daughter fly high up into the moonlit skies.

CHAPTER 6
POLLY'S FIRST FLIGHT

"Hang on tight. Here we go," Alvin said as he tucked his head down and gracefully flew from the ice, across the water, then up towards the moon.

They climbed higher and higher. Polly could feel the cool breeze rushing past her as they floated along the sky. Everything was so beautiful from up here. Abby flew right next to Alvin in complete unison. Polly still couldn't believe it. The stars looked so close. For a moment, Polly thought she could almost reach out and touch them.

The horizon was a magnificent sight as they glided over the moonlit waters. She couldn't believe her dreams were coming true.

"Look, Stormy. We can see for miles."

Stormy was holding onto Abby so tight with his head buried in her feathers. Polly knew he was probably scared to death.

"Stormy, don't be afraid. It's beautiful!" Abby assured him.

Stormy slowly lifted his head out from under Abby's feathers and peeked down at the water.

"Wow, Polly—we are up really high!" he yelled.

He then immediately stuck his head back down into Abby's feathers. His whole body shook with fear.

"Oh, Stormy, don't be such a scaredy-cat. It's amazing," Polly said, chuckling to herself and shaking her head.

She was so overjoyed by the sight of all the water. It seemed so big from up here.

Abby and Alvin continued floating across the sky, not making a single sound. Hours went by, and soon, Polly's eyes got heavy. She didn't want to fall asleep because she wanted to see everything. She looked over, and Stormy was fast asleep on Abby's wings. His face was still buried in her feathers. Eventually, she gave in. She laid her head down on Alvin's back, and slowly, her eyes closed. Abby and Alvin continued to fly, but they too would soon need to rest.

"Abby, I think our passengers are out," said Alvin.

Abby looked over at Alvin and nodded. After flying a little longer. Abby pointed to their favorite island. They would stop there every year on their way to Australia.

It was a small island with minimal trees but enough to keep them covered if a storm came through. Alvin always loved catching the huge fish that seemed to love the reef around the island.

"Time for us to land, Alvin."

Alvin nodded in agreement. So, they both swooped down slowly and landed ever so gently on the sand.

"Let's make a bed out of these leaves for our friends to sleep on tonight," Abby quietly said.

They both slid Stormy and Polly off their backs and onto the makeshift bed, and they stayed sound asleep. Abby and Alvin wrapped each other up with their wings and knelt. Soon, they were also fast asleep.

After some hours, Polly was awake, and she tapped Abby as she said, "Abby! Wake up. I can see the sun off in the distance! It's so beautiful. We have to get going."

Abby and Alvin had only been asleep for a couple of hours. Abby started to wake up. She stood up and stretched her wings out as far as she could.

"Where's Alvin?" Abby asked as she yawned.

"Oh, he said he was going fishing for all of us this morning. He should be back soon. Oh, look, Abby. Here he comes."

Alvin came flying over the trees and landed so tenderly on the sand. "Time for breakfast everyone," Alvin said as he started to count out fish for each of them.

Polly ran over to where Stormy was sleeping. She shook him until he woke up.

"Geez, Polly! Stop shaking me. I'm awake," he said.

He stood up tall and stretched his wings out as far as he could. He then stretched his neck back so far that he fell over backward. Polly burst out laughing.

"Not funny, again, Polly."

"You are so silly, Stormy," Polly said as she wrapped her flipper around her little buddy.

"Come on, Stormy, let's go eat. I'm starving."

Alvin handed them each a leaf with three fish to eat.

"Eat up everyone! We have a big day today."

They all ate every last bit of fish.

"I'm stuffed," said Stormy.

"Me too," said Polly as she rubbed her tummy.

"Alvin, dear, are we ready to fly out?" Abby asked.

"Yes, my darling."

"Okay, you two! Grab your things. It's time to go!"

Abby walked out to the water and used her feathers to flip water all over herself. Then she shook it all off.

"Just washing up. I will be there in a minute," she said.

Polly once again climbed up onto Alvin's back, and Stormy climbed up onto Abby's.

"Hang on, Stormy. Here we go."

Abby jumped up in the air and swooped down over the water. Up they went. Alvin was right behind her. Polly was smiling from ear to ear. Even though it was still slightly dark, Polly could see the sun. She couldn't wait until the sun was shining right on her. She reached straight up at the sky with her flippers.

"Woohoo," Polly yelled.

"Polly, stop that! Hang on tight," Alvin said sharply.

Polly stopped and laid her head down on Alvin's back.

"Abby," Alvin called.

"Yes, Alvin."

"Looks like we have some pretty strong winds and possibly a storm up ahead."

"Oh my! You're right. I think we need to change course for a while."

"Change course?" Polly asked.

"It's just temporary," said Alvin.

Abby and Alvin both swooped off to the left, slightly away from the sun.

"No, we can't go this way," Polly said and started to cry.

Abby flew right up next to Alvin.

"Sweetie, we have to go this way. We won't make it through that storm. Don't worry. We will get back on track in just a little while."

Polly calmed down and nodded her head in agreement. Then she turned away from Abby and continued to stare at the big orange ball in the distance. They flew for what seemed to be an eternity. Stormy was on Abby's back, snoring like he always did; Polly laughed. She was watching everything, and she could see the storm moving off into the distance.

Finally, they started turning once again towards the sun. She could see what seemed to be whales breaching in the distance. She saw dolphins playing tag. *What a beautiful sight to see*, she thought. They were getting closer and closer to the sun. She could finally feel the warm rays against her black feathers. This was something she had been longing for.

Abby and Alvin would swoop down across the water and then fly straight back up again. They did that over and over. It was almost like a roller coaster.

"We are almost there, Polly," Alvin said.

Polly could hardly contain herself. The sun was so big and bright.

"Stormy, look! The sun is out," Polly yelled with excitement.

Stormy slowly lifted his head, pushed his glasses up onto his nose, and peeked over the side of Abby. He then looked down at the water.

"Wow, Polly! This is awesome," he said.

Abby and Alvin continued to float along in the warm breeze. They were barely flapping their wings across the open ocean.

"I see land," Polly screamed.

"Yes, sweetheart! That is Australia," said Abby.

Polly wore the biggest grin ever.

"Stormy, look! It's Australia," she said as she reached down and wrapped her flippers around Alvin.

She then whispered to him, "Thank you, Alvin. Thank you."

Alvin just smiled back at Polly and said, "Your new journey has only just begun."

The Beginning......

ABOUT THE AUTHOR

Beth Moore was born on May 16, 1965. She grew up on a small rural farm in Larue, Ohio. Her parents sold their farm when she was 13 and they moved to Florida where she still lives today. Beth is a daughter, sister, wife , and mother of two boys. After the loss of her oldest son, her love for the outdoors blossomed.

Living in sunny Florida, Beth takes full advantage of the long summer days and warm weather.

She loves to travel to unknown destinations in her motorhome with her husband and her two adorable dogs.

Not only does Beth have a passion for writing, but She also has a love for adventure.

You will most certainly find her sitting on a beach, hiking the Smokies, or enjoying a cup of coffee on a snow-covered mountain.

Diary Notes

Diary Notes

Diary Notes

Diary Notes

Diary Notes